M000239979

FINISHING LINE PRESS

www.finishinglinepress.com

Plenty.

poems by

BeeLyn Naihiwet

Finishing Line Press
Georgetown, Kentucky

Plenty.

ACKNOWLEDGMENTS

List of publications in which poems from Plenty appear:

Kweli Journal: "Clear"

The Halycone: "A Word in the Wild"

The Halcyone/The Black Mountain Press/HerWords: "Growing Up Black with
a Book;" "Grandma's Fool"

Ginosko Literary Journal: "Escape;" "Overwhelm;" "To the Daughter in Wild
Denial;" "Tide;" "Many Years Later You Find Yourself at the Wedding of Your
First and Lost Best Friend;" "Dissonance;" "Rebound;" "Goals;" "Plenty"

Mom Egg Review: "Always this Turmoil" forthcoming

Publisher: Leah Huete de Maines
Editor: Christen Kincaid
Cover Art: Katrina Russell. The Beeches, Christon. BS262xw.
Author Photo: Axum Araya
Cover Design: Emma L. Edwards, The Fine Arts Printing Company LTD.

Order online: www.finishinglinepress.com
        also available on amazon.com

Author inquiries and mail orders:
Finishing Line Press
P. O. Box 1626
Georgetown, Kentucky 40324
U. S. A.

Table of Contents

Forecast..1

Growing Up Black With a Book 2

Crest...3

Parting with a Touch...4

Design..5

Clear...6

Grandma's Fool...7

Escape..8

True Colors...9

A Word in the Wild...10

Echo..12

Genesis...13

Apple..14

Overwhelm...15

To the Daughter in Wild Denial.......................................16

Quality Time..17

My Sister in Struggle...18

Unconscious..19

Judgment Day 20

Home...21

Dear Mama..22

When I Say 23

Let It Rain..24

Glow Girl 25

Access...26

Drip 27

There Comes a Time 28

The Audacity of Tomorrow 29

Insurance 30

For the Moon in You 31

Ebb and Flow 32

Always This Turmoil 33

Tide 34

Water, a Love Story 35

I Know Why They Call It Falling 36

Weep 44

The Witness 45

Many Years Later You Find Yourself at the Wedding of Your
  First and Lost Best Friend 46

Whole 48

Love & War 49

Dissonance 50

Babel 51

Gamble 52

My Brother in Battle 53

Sister 54

Will 55

Daughter 56

Rebound 57

Goals 58

Grandma's Flight 59

Plenty 60

For my mother Askale, who's gone but never left me.

"I am a reflection of my mother's secret poetry as well as of her hidden angers."

—Audre Lorde, *Zami: A New Spelling of My Name*

Forecast

My father doesn't know
about my reverence for water women
or what it means to be one.
Something tells me he would think
the whole thing *ibdan*—craziness,
not unlike how he and his friends sneer
at women who seem insusceptible to
their criticisms and compliments.
As a young woman in need of water I vowed
to only love men who were nothing
like my father, only to fall for the fiery ones.
Nonetheless the other day
my mighty father said to me
casually, as if it wouldn't save us,
mai tmesli—You look like water.

Growing Up Black with a Book

For Maya Angelou

Your winding signature on the hardcover
is moving. My fingers
trace swaying branches, back and forth.
You, a towering willow full of Black life,
descend to grant my request for counsel
and in bowing, rise.
We hang together, sound insights resounding
history coming back to tell itself—
sentencing decorated leaves to their fall.
In great detail you've firmly logged
what makes the streets so mean.

I watch as wooden words bend to your will
and commanding lines form passage
ways for Black girl to play with abandon
on narrow sidewalks in Sunday best.
Over the years your planted seeds sprout
and stick together, rooting
for Black girl turned woman
to outlast ruthless seasons.
The night sky bears witness
to her burden of being
different, reminding her to bloom
and behold,
even the stars look lonesome.

Crest

We unwittingly create another world
whenever our bodies immerse in Black love.
This world of water consumes all
and we go rolling down the river
of each other. I am you and you are mine.
We wade through the wild and take turns
stirring glory.

Parting with a Touch

I realize I could see your goodbye
coming toward me.
You studied my face sadly
with the tenderness of someone
who comes bearing darkness.

I almost missed it,
so relieved to see the softness
return to your eyes.

I searched your face, openly blushing
and unwittingly adding to the weight
of the dying light.

I charmingly implored you,
"Rub my head and I'll close my eyes
and open them to find you gazing lovingly
at me. Okay?"

I can only imagine how I looked to you.

"I don't want to be a burden to you," you said.
I confused it for insecurity.
It wasn't until you dismissed my objections
that I began to understand.

I sat up slowly, tried to take a deep breath.
"What are you trying to tell me?"
But I knew.

I was packing all my things
when you walked back into the room.
You stopped to dry your eyes with a t-shirt
before pulling me into an embrace.

It felt like *Thank you.*

Design

What I thought
was a star
turned out to be
a snake
in the sky.

Clear

In the middle of dinner my little sister reports
her first day of kindergarten was fun except
for the teacher who gave her a brown
crayon to draw a self-portrait.
"I said to her, 'I'm not brown, I'm Black'" Roza says,
adding, "She didn't even know that!"
I feel my father object from across
the table. I don't take my eyes off Roza.
She stands up on her knees in her chair,
her small body barely able to contain her big
ideas. She says that the teacher pointed
to her hair to make the distinction between
the color black and the brown of Roza's skin.
Instantly I picture the classroom scene:
Roza glaring at the teacher, unable
to argue with a lady who clearly knows her colors.
I wait for her to finish chewing
a mouthful of chicken, followed by a long sip
of water. She loves being the center of attention.
I wonder if she knows my heart's in her mouth,
anxious that I hadn't been clear enough
about the complexities of color and race,
and how to tell my father that
the moon made me do it.
Finally she says, "I said, 'Yeah my hair is Black
and I'm Black and my sister is Black and
my family is Black, so I need a Black crayon.'"
She gives a big laugh.

Grandma's Fool

Sometimes I miss my grandmother so much
I can almost bring her back. It's like
she's right in front of me, eyes dancing
and mouth pretending to be bothered
by my relentless longing.

When she was here she'd scold me
for not being self-conscious. My too-often
and too-loud laughter made her cringe
and look around apologetically.

A heavy rain hit the last summer
I visited and my clichéd heart led me to dance
in the street on the way to her house.
Onlookers seeking cover under various
storefronts twisted their faces
in disapproval and concern.

Adey was in her chair when I arrived.
I could tell from her will to be invisible
that the gossip beat me there.
She tried to pull away when I bent to kiss her.
Taking her head in my hands, I planted
several kisses on her face and neck.

Lbi gberi, she said, and I laughed.
Then, "What use is it advising a fool?"
which made me laugh harder.
Suddenly I became aware of how fiercely
I miss her and said so.

"It's you who leaves," she said, before
getting up slowly to make me *shahi.*

Escape

I'm trying to explain addiction
to my father the prodigal son. He's back
to giving advice he wouldn't take.
He now claims that a full understanding
of consequences is a reliable deterrent.
It's not that simple, I say. Addiction is
beyond reason—like love.
Love makes one better, he objects.
Sure, I try again, but addiction is
like unrequited love.
He starts to say something
about *common sense,*
barely catches himself—
like making the last flight out.

True Colors

I can see it all: how we weave
your stories and mine
into a single one
How we come to find *yes* and *you*
in silent touch
How we slowly enter each other's pain,
bearing balm for the wounds and scars

How we take each other back,
show the way
this turn led to that time
and this place became the point
of one more ending
How we go hand in hand to that point
and bless it for its service
to our story

How we breathe life to the dying
and dead in both of us

How we come back to the living
and go deeper into the Now:
its vastness, its dimensions, its true colors—
Black on Black

A Word in the Wild

In the beginning was the word
and it was not enough.
My 17-year-old eyes scanned the waiting room,
trying to lose myself in the wall art.
My focus narrowed in on a poem:
Finding Her Here.
How did I get here?
My few remaining friends
would not be found here.
Soon it will be done
but not over.

I stared at the poem
with a stinging bitterness,
each loving and empowered line
excluding and keeping me out—
on the wrong side of Here.

On the other side a woman found herself
and forgave herself—
an idea so strange it seemed forbidden
and wild enough I heard my name.

Between the lines emerged the woman
with the call of freedom,
arms outstretched into a trail for me.
I drew closer.
A touch on my shoulder and I turned
to find a nurse saying,
We're ready for you now.
I followed behind her.

Had she called me?
Soon we were in front of a door.
In here, she gestured.
Inside I found myself thinking
of the woman on the other side.

I would find her.
She would be waiting.
She had given me her word—
it was plenty.

Echo

If a girl falls in front of family
and nobody hears it,
does it make a sound
for the rest of her life?

Genesis

My father is convinced his eye surgery was conducted
by students for practice. *Melamamedi koyne*, he bristles.
I assure him that he hadn't been an experiment,
that a doctor had in fact done the operation.
He mutters something about having been butchered
as I readjust his pillows. I lie down with my back to him,
texting my brother-in-law for updates on my sister's ongoing labor.
I relay to my father that Baby Number Four is still on the way.
He prays aloud for a safe delivery, then says quietly,
"God really did Woman wrong. That has to be the worst kind of pain.
How does she do it? Work, school, three kids and now another one."
Hayli, I say, she's strong.
"You think it's strength," he disagrees, "I think it's faith."
Sure, I say, it's faith that gives strength.
He makes a sound,
something like suspicious awe.

Apple

Askale's daughter fell in love
with Barbara's son and declared
America beautiful.
Instantly she forgave God the war
that catapulted her small tribal life
into the northwestern corner
of a stable and racist Western society.
The chaotic details of her 23 years
sprang and assembled themselves
into perfect sense on his face.
Suddenly she felt inconvenienced
by space, couldn't imagine
the need for their bodies
not to be in perpetual touch.
Askale's daughter fell in love
so deeply she learned
why they call it falling.

Overwhelm

There's a lot
to be said for love,
said the seed to the fruit,
but sometimes it will
bury you.

To the Daughter in Wild Denial

If your mother dies when you're eleven
you may look for her in other people's mothers
or any older woman who shows
the slightest interest in you.
You may look for her in her sisters
who go decades without calling and later
speak of their impossible grief by way
of explanation and notice of further absence.
You may look for her in your stepmothers
especially the one you call Mama
who introduces you as her daughter and
whose occasional mean streak reminds you
though you never forget that it's in name only.
Years later, you may be surprised when
you realize you'd even looked for her
in the men you loved desperately.
You may look for her in-between lines
of poetry that fill you up until
you burst like a balloon.
You may look for her in a stranger,
in the mirror, in her handwriting on the back
of the photo that you carry around for years.
You may look for her forever
and everywhere except in your father
which is the last place she would be.

Quality Time

My father is in love and I'm angry.
I don't know what I want,
but what I don't want is the stupid
sparkle in his eyes as he video chats with his
spell of a wife, who's younger than I,
which is of course how he likes them.
Never mind that we're at a restaurant.
I make small talk with the waitress,
taking my time to order, as he picks that moment
to give a virtual tour of the place. I smile
to keep from yelling at him to stop neglecting
his years the way he neglects his children.
When I'd told a friend that my father's still
adjusting to being elderly, she'd laughed,
"Your father isn't aging. He's aging you!"
I feel as old as God, who seems to never
take my side. What's a father to do
but show you how it's done.

My Sister in Struggle

Dad kept having kids.
I couldn't stop reading.
You clung to the culture.
I left my diary open.
Your mother was living.
I didn't learn to cook.
You talked back to Dad.
Dad kept having kids.
I talked to God.
You wanted to get married.
I wanted the moon.
You minded your manners.
I ended another relationship.
You became a mother.
Dad kept having kids.
I drank whiskey.
You put your marriage first.
I saw a therapist.
You looked on the bright side.
I talked back to Dad.

Unconscious

You're the only
soft thing in my life,
he says.
The easier to
mold you,
she hears.

Judgment Day

You break my heart with those revolving
doors of eyes and a STOP sign of a smile,
looking like a lost love letter.

I don't know how the world survived
the night its affliction rocked your small body
and you cried, "I'm a dirty girl."

You lay limp in my arms,
my sleeves damp with your tears.
It's okay, I whispered
into your hair, although there's nothing okay
about learning that your skin
is a few shades too dark to be accepted.

I stared into the darkness over your head,
confronting Everything
for assailing your spirit.

It was my anger that summoned God.

Home

Home is that which you lost. Home is, *How could you?* Home is the thing that happened which you never told anyone. Home is the other thing that happened which you never told anyone. Home is protect, not to be confused with protection. Of course you confuse it often, knowingly. Home is not who you are; it's who you love. Home is your mother who feared your father who fears you, who fears those you love. Home is calling home. You are at home less and less; are you homeless? Are you home sick? What's making you sick?

Dear Mama

I look for you everywhere
from the strange to the familiar.
What seems to be you
turns out to be a mirage.
You are nowhere.
Only not.

When I Say

Let's play it by ear
what I mean is, let's get together tonight
and talk about Assata's bold example,
e.e. cummings' wild confessions,
Serena's lively willpower,
the intersection of femininity and feminism,
the poetry of hip-hop,
Prince's reign,
Malcolm's courage,
Obama's touch,
Rumi's transcendence,
Beyonce's brilliance,
all while reviving the art of eye contact.

Let It Rain

Your new relationship is a month old
and you're proud of reaching this milestone.
Somehow you've managed not to run
at the sight of stay in his eyes.
It helped of course that you only committed
to linger, which is different from staying.
Semantics matter, although his touch
matters most, this moon of a man.
You search for the perfect words to describe
the feel of him and keep returning
to water. They say one can go no more
than a week without it and you have
no interest in finding out for yourself.
So you remain without waiting
for this relationship to flow
into the rest of your thirst.

Glow Girl

For Raheal

The sunflower to my moon,
you remind me of carefree summers,
boy bands and lip gloss.

Stop to high dive into dance
on city streets when they play
your song.

Stay wild and free—
What could go wrong
that you won't turn
into glow, girl?

Remember you as you
bring sun to flowers.
Behold and bask
in your precious glory.

Access

All my passwords contain birds.
Funny given my fear of flying,
and my gratitude for grounding work,
which prompts my brother to mock me.
Still birds discreetly appear
to let me into secure spaces.
Once inside, I glance back at them.
But they are nowhere to be seen.
Where do they go, these birds?
What's their secret?
They're teaching me a lesson:
the important distinction
between in and inside.

Drip

Things are going well for my father.
Over coffee he fills me in on his wife's visa approval.
It's your good luck, he concludes decisively.
I scoff, some good luck
that serves others instead of me.
Don't be silly, he says, it's for others
that you need luck—your own journey
is already triumphant.
I don't recognize this version
and say so. He falls quiet, then adds,
When she comes, you'll be free.
My index finger traces the rim of the cup.
So can you go with me, he asks after a while.
Of course. I put his appointment in my calendar.
That's good, he says. I don't correct him.

There Comes a Time

When the one who
should shield you
places the bomb
in your hand.

Don't be afraid
to explode.

having dinner with Mama and her best friend.
y advise me to marry and have children.
y to sell them on OurTime, a dating site for people over 50.
y wave me off and exchange a look that draws a line between them and me.
friend declares that men over 50 don't want them.
ey want young women," Mama adds, as she reaches across the table
ut a second helping of chicken on my plate.
annoyed by their resignation, the ready forfeiture of life after failed marriages.
re have to be women who found love after love,
my father who went on to marry a woman half his age.
ift gears: Okay, never mind men your age; how about younger men?
y laugh and laugh. I look from one to the other in confusion,
n in slow recognition of these artists.
Mama who cries, "Young men, they're too hard in bed!"
y burst into laughter again. I join.

Insurance

Every now and then my sister and I
get into a big fight. This is one of them.
She strikes with cruel reminders.
I return the favor. Fragments of past
shame, guilt and grief fly around us,
picking up pace and cutting us. We retreat
to our respective corners of the couch.
I can hardly sit still—it's how I cope with pain;
she turns into stone. I turn to her,
half expecting to find a statue.
She's in the flesh and says,
"Do you think we'll end up killing each other?"
I think about it. We resent our deep closeness,
the thin line between bond and bondage.
I don't know, I say at last.
I curse my luck—I just know she'll survive.
Our eyes meet. We dare our mother to live.

For the Moon in You

You make me think
of hammocks,
Scripture,
the fullness of ellipses
at three in the morning,
and sweet naps in the afternoon.
I want to feed you
an olive just because
it sounds like love.

You make me think
of Sundays,
Eternal Sunshine,
the language of tinted windows
in the parking lot,
and 90s R&B after midnight.
I want to search you
in the dark only to find
we embody the light.

You make me think
of postcards,
Purple Rain,
the shape of welcome
in the meeting of eyes,
and the witness of the moon.
I want to give you
a life named Black
so you know it's real.

Ebb and Flow

He loved her impossibly
the way night
approaches morning
only to disappear

She loved him completely
the way water
approaches land
without motive

Always This Turmoil

Always this turmoil of what you need
from me, Mama. There's unrest in the unknown
cause of death. You might say
there's unrest in death. Sometimes
I can feel your heart breaking.
You stop coming around.

It's your birthday. First thing this morning
I made love to a man I've been dating
for three months and two days.
I didn't think of you until I was
on my way home from work.

That's awesome, your firstborn replied
when I texted her about your birthday.
Awful, I correct her to myself.

I meant to drink when I got home
and ended up lying in bed,
staring up at the ceiling
until it cracked open.
My eyes narrowed in search of you.
If there's a God, you'd see me
and I wouldn't see you.

Sister came into my room and caught
me hiding from heaven.
"We have to stop being the poor children
who lost their mother. I'm going to celebrate
her instead," she said.

I don't believe her.

Tide

I give him the moon.
He says it invades the night.

I give him the sea.
He says it divides the land.

I give him the garden.
He says it depresses the ground.

I give him the air.
He says it abandons the body.

I give him the poem.
He says it serves the poet.

Water, a Love Story

I write around you
around the fire that's closing in
Maybe I'm pleading with the spirit
of everything to intervene
to keep the flames at bay
to give me more time
to take you away from the searing heat
Let my hand be balm until we've made it
back to the days before the fire started
when my love was greater than the odds
Now my fears intensify and my tears fall
Maybe just maybe they compel the rain
to pour and pour until the fire is out
and you and me stay you and me
living testimony that water works

I Know Why They Call It Falling

1.

Not looking up from the book,
you told me there would be no
cell reception where you were going.
My heart sank
and the water was ice cold.

"What's with the Holocaust?"

you demanded, even colder,
firing without warning.

2.

I found out about
your three-year relationship
a year into ours.
You got a tattoo of my name.
I let it mean too much.

3.

That time I found out you were cheating on me again
I wrote my rage with lipstick
on your windshield.
I felt crazy.

I watched from a distance
as you hopped in the car
and drove right past
the carwash.

Too cool for shame.

4.

We were in New York for the premiere.
I felt threatened by all the beautiful women.
I accused you of inappropriate behavior
and stormed off.

You ran after me, grabbed my arms,
pushed me against the fence
in the parking lot.

Later you'd write and apologize for
"touching you wrong."
Your tone was soft,
unlike your hands.

5.

It was the day before Valentine's Day.
"I am no longer in love with you."
I fell to the floor.
You offered me water,
a ride, advice.

The way one might someone
who said she was depressed
only to later learn
she took her life.

6.

The only birthday I remember
celebrating with you,
you said, "you were born for me."

Words so sweet,
when I was most bitter.

7.

Funny how I love you
also means
goodbye.

8.

You jumped into the passenger seat.
I drove recklessly.
I was yelling, "Why? Just tell me why!"

You begged me to stop the car,
promised to tell me the truth.
I did.

"Sometimes, I just want to fuck somebody."

You waited for me to react.
I was thinking that I couldn't kill myself
over you, after all.

9.

By way of explanation,
you said you had been looking for me
in other women.
That made sense enough.
What didn't make sense
was that you knew exactly
where I worked. But then again,
there is no creativity in that.
And you are, before lover,
an artist.

10.

In an email you referred to me
as your "friend and future."

It is only now that I recognize
in those words
how it came to be,
over and over,
that you were hardly
here.

11.

All your lovely emails
all your words of devotion
are now in a folder called
"Receipts."

12.

I found a CD you made for me.
On the cover you wrote:
"I feel so much love for you. I won't let you down."

What's love
got to do with it?

13.

What's worse?

That you shaped words
into a relationship
or that I mistook your words
for you?

14.

I once had a dream
that we had a son named Will.
We both agreed that Will and not William
was a good name.
I thought about Will for years,
thought the dream was a glimpse
into our future.

One broken day, God spoke to me.
He said Will was my own.
I refused to listen.
I needed him to be ours.

15.

You once said that I was to you
what air is.
I replied that the word "almost"
made me think of you.
You were offended, said I sought
to reject and dismiss.

But we both knew
insult was no match
for injury.

16.

The last time I saw you
we were both crying.
You said you didn't think
we could ever not cry.

So beautiful a sentiment
I forgot we were crying
for different reasons.

17.

The reunion after three years
I was so nervous standing outside
that hotel room.
I couldn't handle seeing your face again.
You had to talk me down
from the other side
of the door.

18.

Three years later I returned
to find my clothes still hanging
in your closet just as I'd left them.

You watched me as I touched each one.
I turned to you slowly. Your face.
It was your face, but
it was every thing.

19.

We used to fight all the time.
My insecurities and trauma showed up.
You met them with frustration and anger.

We found a card for a counselor taped to our mailbox.

We bonded over being offended
and left it taped for the neighbors
to see.

20.

That Halloween we decided to be "racial stereotypes"
you combed out my hair
until we had matching afros
and wore sweat suits with one pant leg rolled up.

You took many pictures of me.

I never felt so seen.

21.

I was committed
to defending our love.
I objected to my therapist's comments
about our "power dynamic" and your
"way with women."

I criticized her inability to grasp
that we could never truly
leave each other.

"Can he be more left?"

You left me
defenseless.

22.

Everyone wrote in an
'All About Me' journal for my birthday once.

I came across your message:
"remember when we...remember??"

I remember wishing you'd written
something more meaningful.

23.

We fell in love
at first sight
and fell deepest
in fits of laughter.
I will love again
I suppose,
but my laugh
didn't survive
us.

24.

"Until the stars drown,"
you told me

a lie.

Weep

The world is on fire.
You're made of water.

Rush, love.

The Witness

Of all the women in me
the granddaughter
is bravest;
the daughter, keenest;
the sister, strongest;
the friend, wisest;
the lover, freest;
the professional, kindest;
and the poet, truest.

Many Years Later You Find Yourself at the Wedding of Your First and Lost Best Friend

You look out into the dance floor where she radiates surrounded by her forever best friends, all of whom are your former friends except for one who dared (or cared) to somewhat remain in your life. You're happy for the shining bride and this capacity makes you happy for yourself. One of your older sisters sits next to you and, following your gaze, asks: *Can you believe they stayed close all these years?* Her tone registers surprise and disdain on your behalf. Instantly you're transported to the years since you were all seventeen. Back to that fateful day a cute boy who turned out to be twenty-two said you looked like a queen even though you were awkward and wore braces and happened to be standing next to one of the prettiest girls. How you came alive in that moment for the first time since your mother died six years earlier. How each red flag looked like a light at the end of the tunnel. How you swallowed your will for three years. You slipped into a world so lewd and lawless it served a savage God.

You escaped that world broken and bound by every terrible knowing. Your friends long gone with their carefully crafted reputations intact. Their close-knit two-parent families agreed with each other that their wholesome daughters were to keep their distance from you who knew wolves intimately. Neither welcome nor worthy, you became a warning. Your prideful father became bitter that you dashed his hopes of a trophy daughter. You apologized for falling prey to a man who saw your pain. Everywhere you turned you were That Girl who lost her senses, That Girl who was the shame of her father—a man prone to patronizing, That Girl who had seen too much to be harmless. You encountered a world so narrow and rigid it served a small God.

You departed from that world damaged and you grieved every dream you ever had. You wandered aimlessly for years before incidentally making a home out of the kindness of strangers, lines of poetry that lingered on your skin, the example of trees, and your own tenacity. You settled in. Later, you set out to create a world of women who had been That Girl. You roamed the wilderness of your becoming and rested in the water of your being. You grew to welcome and embrace all That Girls in you and bore witness to discarded others in sisterhood. You embodied a world so gracious and boundless it served a true God.

You return to the wedding. The stunning bride and groom dancing closely as the bridesmaids and groomsmen follow their lead. *Yes, I can believe it,* you respond to your sister at last. The scene in front of you makes effortless sense to you. What feels incredible, and what you couldn't have imagined as That Girl, is becoming this woman watching your long lost friends glitter together and who is suddenly filled with strange and blessed gratitude for everyone who ever left or counted you out and inadvertently served your audacious journey of self-discovery from scarce to plenty. You catch the bride's bright eyes and raise your glass in her honor from a deep place within you where God looks on proudly.

Whole

Because you learned long, long ago
that you are neither small nor superior.
You wear your vulnerability openly.
They don't know what to do with you.
A woman who is plenty.
Divine by default.

Love & War

For the third time this afternoon
my father asks how long I'll be away.
"Look, I took care of rent for next month,"
I defend myself. He's unarmed.
I keep dodging. Soon I deliver
an impassioned internal speech about
self-care as necessity.
That's not it, he says, *It's just that everything
goes dark for me when you're not around.*
Instantly I'm wounded.

Dissonance

It occurred to her that perhaps novels
were to blame for her fanciful ways.
She had taken those grand gestures to heart,
blurring the line between art and life.
And when the men came,
she would confuse intensity for intimacy,
connection for compatibility,
and vulnerability for integrity.
She had followed her wild heart everywhere.
This time she would stay put,
attend to her regained senses,
dressed in fine disillusion—
not unlike the dumb plot
doomed to thicken.

Babel

My father is trying to console me
with platitudes. I interrupt him.
"I know it'll pass, but right now
I'm brokenhearted, okay?"
He continues, *You can't give up*
like this. You can't give in to defeat.
I want to scream, but have no energy.
I just know my chest will collapse
if I speak above a whisper.
"I'll be fine," I manage.
He commands that I remember who I am,
Everyone turns to you for support—
another poor defense against despair.
He adds, *You must not surrender.*
A soldier never quits.
I can't take any more,
"This isn't war, Dad; it's love."
Gently, he breaks it to me:
There is no greater war.

Gamble

We lovers can be reckless with love. We think we worship love so much
if love calls, we'd drop everything and run toward it. But we underestim
our recklessness, the roots we plant as we wait to be called. We don't e
realize that we're making love wait. And when love calls, we mistake
ambivalence for caution. We expect love to understand. We don't expe
to look like loss.

My Brother in Battle

I was a junior and you a freshman when
the wickedness of the world caught up to us
and we learned that my crush and yours had
become an item. We walked home from school
in silent procession. That evening we lie on
opposite ends of the living room couch,
cursing their union with increasing fervor.
We felt injured and insulted individually and
decided that this pairing was equally an offense
against our collective as brother and sister.
United by our wounds, we vowed to deprive
our respective crushes of our friendship.
We'd make them pay for overlooking us
and choosing each other. The next morning
we walked to school with great intensity as if
going into war. We were not deterred by the fear
that our plan of attack might backfire.
The only thing that mattered then was that
we were in it together and would fight
side by side. Some things never change.

Sister

In my favorite memory of us
you fumed and cursed
the world and its lack of fairness.
I beamed as I was falling
for a friend who later became a stranger.

"There's no hope for real change!"
You paced the floor, seething.
I edited a text of thinly veiled desire
into ambiguity, tried to pace myself.
Be mindful of the energy you put out
into the universe, I said absently.

"Oh shut up, you fake Buddhist!"

I burst into laughter.
You couldn't help but join.
We laughed and laughed
as if we'd needed
a good long cry.

Will

What's fire
to water women
who spring
out of ashes?

Daughter

For Yerusalem Moore

There's much written about your troubles.
You'll know that you're not alone and
will overcome like others before you.
This is your work. But there's more
to life, more to you than surviving
close calls. Life also gives you cherries.
It's possible to get it right on your first try.
L is for long-lost *and* long-lasting,
and not every day needs saving.
There are times when the light is at the
beginning of the tunnel. Remember:
You're as much sun as you are daughter,
and just as likely to suffer a setback
as to stir the sky.

Rebound

Love, n. A high voltage fan with variable speeds.
Love, n. The sky, a blanket.
Love, n. The number 1, denoting a beginning.
Love, n. The time between purchase of a lottery ticket and checking the results.
Love, n. An unlikely friendship.
Love, n. A window.
Love, n. An unpopular opinion.
Love, n. The last parking spot.
Love, n. The kindness of strangers.
Love, n. Blind spots.
Love, n. The moon, a witness.
Love, n. Self-diagnosis.
Love, n. Quiet.
Love, n. The shadow of an idea.
Love, n. Baby's breath.
Love, n. The world at 4:00 am.
Love, n. Water.
Love, n. Blackness.
Love, n. Moss.
Love, n. The poetry of traffic.
Love, n. The color purple.
Love, n. The hoodie.

Goals

Aim for heaven
in every encounter,
or something
more rare.

Grandma's Flight

Lately I've been noticing trees,
the firmness of their roots,
the length of their reach.
Many nights I've turned
to the moon for company
and was met with reflection.

In the day my eyes dart across the sky,
zigzagging through the clouds
as though I'm late
for an appointment.
The wind, at times, seems to relay
a message I can't quite make out—
something about a sign.

The morning I heard you passed away,
I went down to the lake
and sat on a wooden bench.
The ground held me
as I peered into the water.

A large white bird flew over and perched
itself on the back of the bench.
It waited perfectly still as I
continued searching the waves.
When I turned to it,
the bird gave a slight nod.

Plenty

What's better than ascension?

Boundlessness.

ADDITIONAL ACKNOWLEDGMENTS

Thank you to my sister/self Weyni "Nalem" for every sacrifice you made to keep my dreams alive—you have always been my hero and my home. Thank you to my sisters Berizaf, Raheal and Axum for loving me whole in the wilderness and inspiring me with your beautiful courage. I write for all my sisters, always, in solidarity. Thank you to my brothers Belay, Aaron and Alem for showing me the various faces of love. Thank you to my father Araya for raising the fighter in me and for all the parables. Thank you to Mama, Kiros for being there and making room for me. Thank you to my best friend Feben Ghirmatzion for being true and long-lasting—blessed to be "Godfriends" since time immemorial. Thank you to my "President of All Things Naihiwet" Tirhase Haddis who supports me with wild abandon. Thank you to my dear friends Christopher Blue, Christina McRae, Mekonnen G-Mariam, Sabina Neem, Grace Weigel, Jennifer Pinner, and Konrad Volz for seeing me, for staying and sharing your be-ings with me. Thank you to Joy Roulier Sawyer for insisting that I am a poet long before I could believe it. This book could've never happened without your teaching, encouragement and friendship. Thank you, too, for writing *Lifeguards*. Thank you to Natalie J. Graham for your poems and time. Thank you to Jayne Relaford Brown for writing the poem "*Finding Her Here*," for finding me years ago and guiding me here. Thank you to my late mother, Askale and my late grandmother, Adey—the original water women of my life.

BeeLyn **Naihiwet** is a Seattle-based Black poet. Born in Ethiopia, she immigrated to the U.S. as a refugee with her family when she was ten. She's the middle child of her late mother's three children, and the fourth of her father's fourteen. This often results in her being mistaken for the mother of her youngest siblings—an idea she only occasionally corrects.

BeeLyn holds a BA in Creative Writing and a MA in Counseling Psychology, and fell in love with poetry when she discovered Rumi in a college Medieval Literature class. She's been greatly influenced by the work of many poets, among them Nikki Giovanni, Lucille Clifton, Marie Howe, and Wislawa Syzmborska. Her poetry appears or is forthcoming in *Kweli Journal, The Halcyone, Ginosko Journal,* and *Mom Egg Review.*

In addition to her love for poetry, BeeLyn is deeply committed to the practice of bearing witness. In her personal life, as well as through her work as a licensed mental health provider, she advocates for destigmatizing mental health challenges—particularly in the Black community. She is also passionate about empowering women.

When she was twenty, BeeLyn moved to Washington, DC for two years, where she felt free and affirmed in her Blackness. After returning home to Seattle, she held close these validating experiences as she navigated both personal and professional spaces that challenged her unapologetic presence and voice.

After years of struggling to reconcile her Ethiopian and American cultures and identities, BeeLyn created a home in the tension that exists between them. She gave herself the name Naihiwet, which means "of Life." In this name she finds room for her many selves.

BeeLyn is never *not* hoping for rain. She's likely to buy anything with either the word *moon* or its image. She's an introvert and a Virgo, and fully identifies with both. Her most prized possession are her journals, in which she began writing at age eleven. BeeLyn's favorite place to create is on a quiet wooden bench at a park that overlooks the water.

CPSIA information can be obtained
at www.ICGtesting.com
Printed in the USA
FSHW011153020321